Tapestry

Jan Coulter

'For Michelle Alice Ogilvie'

Contents

3 Leaves

Out of my journal

they fell,

3 leaves, pressed

between thoughts.

Pigment altered, from

brilliance to burnished.

Did they absorb my writing?

Will they now speak,

in melody or in anguish,

in poetry or in prose?

In earnest, they listen,

to my breath.

A Balanced Composition

An old pulley, hangs
8 feet high, above
fields of grasses, bronze and green.

A carrying beam, 6 inches square, of Corten steel,
is guided by a cable of twisted iron cord.
From this structure, suspends a

metal hasp with cotter pin,
securing a heavy horseshoe clasp, grasping
the axis of this bevelled pulley,

rusted, pitted and pocked; resting in tones of sepia, ocher, and
colours for which I have not names. Tinges of
scarlet and vermilion, adorned with streaks of guano,

decorate this piece of 'art' that embodies
strength and purpose; although, I am content,
knowing not its function.

A balanced composition in its symmetry, a
faculty and occupation of considered mechanics,
photographed, in an abandon train yard.

A Beginning

For Sue and Kenny

Every so often,
a moonbeam,
reaches down and
touches our core.

Senses caressed;
meeting of minds, gifted to
accept connection, a
stroke from the heavens.

In such fortune,
embrace is reciprocal, a
joining of souls,
enduring obstacle and barrier.

Absorb this gift,
it will transform and
nurture heart's awakening;
a beginning, sustained.

An Invitation

I want to write about an emotion,
that cannot be touched,
about a tearing of sinew,
for a thousand reasons,
searing a path to the surface.

I want to write about a melody,
dancing, upon the err of reason.
Song of time, absorbed into the
tether that binds our thought,
drawn into the intellect of meter, a

rhythm, scarce and fleeting; the
interval between sleep and prayer.
I want to write about strength, a
beckoning that sets us free,
an invitation to look within.

And so, I write, with
knowledge held inside, that
dare not speak its purpose; while
quiet night, harbours a
yearning, to listen, to the wind.

A Moment's Blur

Red fox,

vibrant coat,

stealthily approaches

roadside shoulder,

amidst traffic's whir —-

grabs her prey

with caution,

disappears;

a moment's blur,

of colour bold.

And Then

Held,
within the view of
memory.

Dare to encroach
upon a recollection, where
stringed instruments speak.

Voice gives colour.
Sound yields rich,
sepia tones,

into which there is birth,
unto which there is surrender.
Fades this gaze of memory, as

candle begins to snuff,
the tangible sifts to dust;
and then . . .

Autumn Vignette

Bark, long ago,
slid away, leaving
skeletal old tree,
naked and smooth.

Weather bruised limbs, stretch
outward, offering purchase,
rest and refuge to
winged creatures.

Bulrushes stand,
bronze blades upright,
perfect cover for
Bittern's silent pose, while

water bugs, legs splayed, as
outriggers or oars,
skate across brackish waters,
whose banks house tiny frogs of Spring.

Poplars, surround this vignette,
moss adorns northern exposure, while
leaves hold hands, dancing, laughing,
within the breath of fall.

Beating Heart

In each other's arms,

entwined,

tangled hair,

upon the pillows,

listening,

to each other's

beating heart.

Being 7

When I was 7, fast approaching 8,

I refused to move, with my Father's new job,

unless, I could take my swing.

Of course, that meant taking the tree also!

20 years ago, I planted a silver maple,

who's branches seem ready now,

to love my swing, and me.

Once again my feet will fly,

high up into her branches,

setting my soul free, to remember

being 7, fast approaching 8.

Beyond the View

I lie down,
with the quiet of your teaching,
close to rotting timbers, of
old bridge, split and sagging.

I drink in your soft verse,
your gentle demeanour.
I see my reflection,
in your limpid, lazy pools.

There are memories here;
for I have been before,
watching leaves swim, in your
pebbled rich stream as

light filters in dappled lit breaths,
stroking pitcher plant and wintergreen.
Lichen adorn old wood and rock, while
mosses beckon bare feet.

You have taught me well.
You have taught me vision,
 beyond the view.

Break the Mould

To be less isolated,
to break the mould,
requires stamina; a
power held close. Reach in,
extricate from jail, the
grip of shyness.

Stretch mind and intellect, to
walk a path unknown.
Travel the rocks of inexperience, and,
in seclusion, find peace.
Strength resides, quietly waiting
to be summoned.

Shed masks, that
serve you not.
Cast off the veneer of caution.
Welcome day's promise; while
mornings are rebirth,
nights, will set you free.

Candle Lit Memory

I give gentle kisses in memory,
to float your dreams,
into dawn.

A quiet stroke,
feels heart's breath
and night's ease.

Fingers run through
tasseled hair, as
slate grey eyes soften; yet,

my soul, dark as onyx,
misses you, in this
candle lit light of night.

Candle Lit Studio

Odd thing,

sitting up all night,

listening to Baroque intervals,

in candle lit studio,

at a desk I made,

with a precise hand,

from a previous time,

of a not forgotten trade.

Cello

The scent of fall,
nuzzles through
window ajar;

stopping to grace
brow, and caress all
senses acute.

Sounds of evening,
transport to place,
centred, calm, yet

travels the mind,
frequently lost.
May Autumn's breath

wrap music's tone
around loss and grief.
May we rest, while

cello wafts a
minor key, to
sooth an aching heart.

Circle of Seasons

I walk through a
thousand leaves,
descending from
Summer's dress, to
Autumn's fecund soil.

Ash yellow,
maple's rainbow, and
supple leathered oak,
mix with nutmeg browns,, of
birch and beech.

White pines shed
blankets of tender needles,
spruce; a bounty of cones,
sustaining fodder, for
creatures of the wild.

And now the rains,
backlit with afternoon sun,
squeezed dry by clouds of grey, while
crisp air introduces Fall.
Cycle of sleep, cycle of seasons.

Courage

It takes courage just to be yourself,

to be the only footsteps in the snow,

loving shadows on a winter's night,

losing yourself, in an Andrew Wyeth painting,

enjoying sheep in a dory, crossing the inlet,

or houses tethered by four corners, against the wind.

Such courage is easy, when it makes you smile.

Crow

At water's edge,
thick knees bent,
supporting legs, thin and stick like.
Talons arch to gain purchase,
in salt infused sand, and approaching tide.

You stare at crustaceans, emerging
from wet grained bubbles.
Your reflection,
even more beautiful;
drawn with brush of morn,

prominent, in full detail,
mimicking to perfection, your gaze.
Such beauty presents, a fleeting image,
erased by advancing waters,
as sun breaks into dawn.

Days Defined

I am a tucked in child.
My shirt is tucked in, the
ends of my tie; tucked in.
Knee socks pulled up
beyond their stretch.

Shoes polished and spit on
to harden a finish, gleaming.
Tunic length, above the knee,
precisely, four inches,
when kneeling.

Bells ring for every event.
Uniform inspection,
morning walk;
mandatory, come rain or sleet,
or environmental disaster!

The order of repetition;
My education.
My years of youth.
My routine.
My days defined.

Deer Toes

Mountain, valley,
scrub and scree,
earth to grave, an
ice coating glistens.

High among the tree tops
scatters snow, like a
dusting of flour, yet a
silent sparkle shines through.

Quiet, this beauty, so absent of sound,
only crow announces herself,
with whir of wing,
passing my vision; intent.

A calm hush, filters
into an escape of time, where
deer toes indent the cold
rich canvas of a winter's morn.

Downward I Clamber

I am dwarfed and hidden,
inside your shadow.
My own, diminished
by the rhythm of
your majestic presence.

For you are mountain, and I
valley, river bed and scree.
I take refuge inside
your foothills, and
hide within your coulees.

Drawn to climb your highest ledge, but
downward I clamber, to
glacial waters, aqua blue, where
Pika play, and I,
exist not in solitude.

Exhale of Summer

Shrivelled, hanging,
tenuously by stems, leaves
cling to their protector.

Reluctant to lose their Summer's dress,
soon left gaunt and naked,
trees brace for Winter's chill.

In Maple's glade,
a crescendo of colour,
swirling about my feet.

And so this season,
arrives on the exhale of Summer,
colours of the Fall, a cycle complete.

Expression

For Wayne Boucher

Charcoal, conte
pastel and oil;
media of emotion, that

paints with language,
spoken in dialects,
assembled fragments; a collage.

Drawn with breath.
Breathe through the
bottoms of your feet,

deep and long and
sustaining, as your mark,
endures time . . .

Fedora

A most striking entrance,

you, and your satin skin,

adorned with jewellery gold,

smile to welcome,

under stunning broad brimmed fedora,

rich and sassy and purple.

Statement of arrival, an announcement,

exuding confidence and comfort,

on this, a grey December day.

For Those Gone Before

Morn for those gone before,
in quiet contemplation.
Though the burden is heavy,
we remember.

There is discomfort in loss.
We name it grief, and
grief is fear, yet,
we remember.

A smile, broad and generous,
echo of voice, a gentle touch,
with laughter shared, open and full,
we remember.

Desire one more conversation,
yearn for comfort and understanding,
a hopeful expectation, as we remember
those gone before.

Funeral

Somber, down turned faces;
some looking outward to greet
old friends, smiling, and a few
ill at ease.

Congregation of peers,
country folk,
keepers of the farm,
keepers of the land.

Not a farmer am I,
neither blood, nor
distant relative, yet,
I morn.

Loss to a community,
loss to an era,
loss to the very fabric
of our valley.

Gaza

Plumes of smoke rise,

from a city,

who once slept.

Now, beneath

piles of rubble,

below which,

her residents lie;

a deep repose,

that never rests.

Geese

Pouring rain

here on the farm,

three ponds,

a trickling brook;

yet you delight

in puddles,

smack in the middle,

of our country road!

Gift of Melody

Phrase of music,
liquid word,
seeps out from
corners of the mind,

that weep, but
for a moment, when
full measure of song,
reaches the soul.

Uplifted, absorbed
into the tapestry of
thought; listen,
to the gift of melody.

Graveyard

Wind listens,
to the moaning of
tombstones, who speak
through darkness, under
rustle of low hanging willow.

A soul is about to
break away, from their
liminal sleep, beneath
markers of marble and
granite, rough and polished.

Rare is awareness, to
witness the freedom of
spirits, gathered in chorus, to
praise their solitude, in the
solemnity of voice.

Half A Heart

Is half a moon
as bereft as
half a heart?

I wonder, does
she weep?
Does she ache

inside her orbit?
Stars gaze with comfort, yet
I sense sorrow.

Days pass, spent and gone.
I look to evening sky, where
moon rises, now full,

neither sad or grieving, but
radiant and whole,
able to comfort, that half a heart.

Hands of Time

At work, they hold their tools,
secure, yet relaxed.
Instruments, balance
deftly in arch and grasp, a
craft man's knowledge of motion.

Square nails, strong fingers,
confident, in their journey,
weave a single strand of wool,
across wrists of strength;
beauty captured in a moment's glance.

Honoured work of ancestors
replicate a teaching,
etched in memory,
repetition with age;
hands of time.

I Am Unsure

Unsure am I,
as to what moves me more;
the many visions presented,
to study, to drink their essence,
detail, rich and full—

Or the mere delight in
having such choice of
awareness paid, to the excitement
of all senses, alerted,
seeking attention.

I Don't

I don't polish

the brass anymore.

Old and tarnished,

like me;

I rather think,

we like it,

this way . . .

I Have A Passion

I have a passion
for old barn hinges,
hasps and handles.

It is their patina,
metal rusted,
bent and twisted,

creaking or silently fixed,
to worn and
silvered barn board,

that attracts my attention.
Their surface, pocked and pitted,
with season's measure;

forged of a period,
crafted to precision,
an era past, a rhythm of time.

Yes, I have a passion for
things, old, worn, and bent.
Perhaps, they remind me, of me . . .

Into the Dawn

Fog so thick,
I cannot see,
from whence I came.

Morning wafts a sweet pungent scent,
of barn and livestock,
hay and manure.

Trees sport a gossamer sheen,
atop fronds still heavily
laden, with snow's mantle.

It is silent, and all is still,
save solitary crow,
drifting through this veil.

Only my footsteps advance,
quietly, methodically,
into the dawn.

January Thaw

Mountain run off,

laughs and chortles,

as it frees itself,

from the stricture

of a frozen bondage.

Three silent crows, watch

as I pass through, this

gentle, January thaw.

Keep The Order

Above the streets,
a desolation.
Windows blown out,
curtains hang in shreds,

sucked out, in the
vacuum of blasts.
An insurrection of
mortar and drone.

On streets below these
ravaged buildings tall;
pepper spray, tear gas, and batons
keep the order . . .

Such a dichotomy
Such a contradiction
Such is war.

Liminal Capture

I wake to farm's melody.
Rooster contributes to this, but other song;
a dearth of music in my woods.

Neither is there breeze,
only calm and quiet.
Perhaps, a liminal place, has

drawn me into this mystery,
where time is absorbed
into the dawn of day.

Perhaps this liminal venue,
might also capture breath,
to float my soul, through this silence.

Limits of the Mind

Equipped with acute hearing,
a musician's blessing, yet not a
player of instruments, or
writer of notes am I.

Blessed with artist's gifts, yet
unable to render an image.
Awareness keen, with line and texture,
I drink in shapes.

Honoured with silent vocabulary,
words trapped upon exit, when
expression is called to speak.
Mute vapours ride on ethers passing,

constricted, and contained.
Quiet travel sees the colour of sound,
hears shape, as graphite speaks
her story upon parchment.

Perhaps a solitary journey, but the
view is rich and sustains,
trapped only by
limits of the mind.

Lobster Boat

Above the bank,
of river, not so wide,
a wooden lobster boat,
rests upon her keel.

Summer grasses nearly
conceal her structure.
Weathered and worn is she,
of peeling pigment, once bold.

Hull, an old marine red, with
body blue, of a water reflected sky.
The wheel house is ash grey,
lashed by elements harsh, over time.

Curious, such a vessel to be a
river craft at all, and to be resting,
upon such a ridge so high;
abandoned by years gone by.

I imagine her crew to be
foxes, who den within, or
gophers burrowing beneath her shelter.
Comforting to know, she is not alone . . .

Lure of Music

I marvel at the power, of
music to transport,
our willingness to follow,
without question or resistance,
to ride the base and treble clef of time.

Melody navigates the mind,
manoeuvres through
heart's filters and
we appear,
a soul, soothed.

Lured to this place
of understanding,
beyond conscious thought
of journey,
we arrive.

Hands touch.
Hearts hold and embrace euphony.
Sound speaks of
warmth and magic; this,
the lure of music.

Meter of Song

Lights, on the boardwalk,
softly shine,
a mile away;

casting a playful glow,
a dance of illumination,
stretched out, upon

watered pockets, the
tide left behind,
quivering in the breeze.

Surf crests white, sky stitches
greys together; ocean's tablet,
woven with kelp and sea grass.

Listen to the meter of song,
who speaks into the wind.
This, the language of the sea.

Minus Twelve Celsius

Chortling,

gurgling,

water;

laps between

bulrush, and

brittle grasses bronze,

delights, in

frigid dawn, and the

cracking of

all things moist and

freezing.

Moments By The Sea

Sand slips
beneath feet, as
tide waxes and wanes.

Crushed rock, like time, cannot be held;
arranged in patterns of beauty,
grains of beach — precision.

Life slips between events,
until dust claims the
last words of wonder.

Moments by the sea;
constant in the care of heart,,
constant in the care of mind.

Morning Walk

Cold as a witches wit,

where snow sparkles and

squeaks under boot.

Pond's overflow, slides

beneath a canopy of ice.

Blue Jays disperse,

caw of crow, sounds, high in

skeletal black locust,

Juncos scatter, amongst the bracken

as Woodpecker

probes an industrious,

Good morning.

Night's Muse

I begin to come to terms with a
hiatus from writing.
Sitting at my desk, I listen to a
collection of Bach's adagios.

Wool socks pulled on,
windows adjusted downward, while
moon drifts through an indigo sky,
night greets with all her possibilities.

Crisp and clean the air.
For a solitary actor, the stage is set.
Clarinet and cello, ease a soul spent.
I drink in their dulcet tones.

Inside the mind,
a place beyond grasp.
Rational thought, struggles to deliver the key,
that only I hold so close.

Unlock the river, where
words flow and are carried
with the current, to enhance the dawn.
Let go the key.

November Day

Between slats of

Venetian blind,

I squint to notice

singular crow,

atop solitary tree.

Its plaintive caw,

blends with ashen sky;

perfect composition,

perfect palate, on this,

a November day.

Obsolete

Printing press of the past,
etches an image, upon the minds,
left to appreciate;
a trade obsolete.

Weigh and mix pigment,
the precision of colour,
paper stock, cut according to grain;
a trade obsolete.

Fingers and hands,
stained with ink, permanent
as your gift, indelible,
a trade obsolete.

October's Witness

Massive are the rocks, smooth and grey,
lashed over time with ocean's rhythm, and
weather's harsh stroke.

Slabs of granite sport lichens and mollusks.
Declivities worn in their surface, yield pools,
where muscles and periwinkles cling.

In these sun warmed baths,
wind whipped tides bring sustenance to these
crustaceans, as surf slides back to

churning waters, smoothing rock as it
recedes and ebbs; yet to dash again,
upon this stone; to thrash and heave.

Orchestra Sounds

Stars laugh upon the water,
back lit, by yellow and amber
lights, of town nearby.

Waves surf in,
to caress beach sand, as
kelp rides the foaming force.

Heavy dew reaches under porch;
coats railing, rocking chair, and me.
I want to sit, the steps are slick.

Inside, a ticking wall clock
slowly breathes with
metronome rhythm as

tide advances, in
similar measured meter; an
orchestra sounds beneath each crest.

Phoenix Rises

Is it the quiet
silence of the damned, heard
upon the midnight air?

Is it the lost, who
weep inside a mind, which
cannot forget?

Phoenix rises above, with
absolute strength,
beyond rebuke,

Rises, free to know, and to
discover, a precious
second chance.

Power of Boundary

I struggle to articulate,
aching words,
stuck in transit,

inside a boundary,
where passage is closed,
limiting negative thought.

Boundary is castle, with
moat and drawbridge,
closed in caution,

to emotions of the day, which
disallow the battering ram of life
to walk with intent.

Boundary is padlock,
fencing robust, keeping in
what we don't want, out,

with gates,
keeping out,
what we don't want in.

Boundary nurtures.
Boundary is strength.
Boundary is power.

Recluse

At market, busy and loud,
he stands apart;
singular, amid the crowd.

Eyes silent,
shoulders slumped, with
body bent,

his presence, reserved.
Shy of demeanour, wearing
veils, behind which to hide,

I sense a furtive mind,
profound sadness and
a weeping heart.

So taken with this view,
I find, that I,
am weeping too.

Rhythm

Feel the sound

of tides.

Hear the surf,

wax and wane.

Taste salt

upon fingers.

Smell kelp,

the air, and witness
.
the rhythm of the sea.

Rock Doves

Water towers, on

roof tops tall, of

buildings planted, on

cobblestone roads,

where newspapers swirl,

in alleys dark,

in New York City,

who never sleeps, while

the rock doves coo.

Rush Hour

Elevator opens to a hollow foyer,
its contents, packed like sardines;
day's work force, anxious for home.

Wind and rain buffet,
a five o'clock drizzle,
inside an afternoon's fading light.

People rush, overcoats drip,
umbrellas open, concealing faces, and the
street car screeches by,

on grid locked roads,
where bicycles swerve, avoiding
trolley's steel track.

Head and tail lights sparkle,
squinting through water drops.
City lights reflect vibrant images,

lurking in puddles, on wet, slick pavement.
A city in waiting for the next shift.
A city speaking the language of sound and colour.

Secret Silence

Light disappears early these days,
darkness shudders stealthily
across valley, hummock, and scree.

The bone factory of trees,
skeletal and naked, pull the
cloak about their shoulders, as it

drops to their knees, caressing toes.
Cool is dark's air, speaking heavily as
day's warmth, percolates in fading breaths;

melding, joining, in exhale of sister fog.
Fall's remnants swirl, lean and gaunt,
blending with the gentle arrival of crystals white,

that beckon and seduce the
promise of dawn, as I listen, to the
secret silence, of the night.

Shadow

Rest, I will not,
in the shadow you
left behind, where
dark is night and
crickets sing.

I'll not lie down inside the
shape of your memory, its
essence touching my skin;
your spirit absorbs into
every nerve ending.

Within my own boundary,
I learn to stand,
outside its stricture.
My image yields a strong truth, and
my feet, are well rooted in time.

Shadow speaks of permanence;
it waxes and wanes in the
presence and absence of light.
In darkness it holds us close,
in light, it holds us complete.

Shadows Long

In fields below,
setting sun, makes shadows
long, of late afternoon.

Fence posts drenched in
light, become beacons in line,
set apart from bracken bronze and

Mullen rusts. Light of fall,
rests on the cusp of
winter's sleep.

Shadows long, late
in the day, await the
break of another dawn.

Silence Shatters

Your comments,
sharp and caustic.
The rebuke, weathers not
within my heart.

Speech mute,
locked in my mind.
From my lips, language
will not form.

Silence shatters conversation.
Chest strung taut, an
instrument tuned to snap.
The orchestra plays a discordant note.

Struck dumb,
my breathing catches in
the corners of my eyes,
which leak, hot and searing.

Standing straight,
my legs force a forward motion.
I leave behind, a muted soul,
dusted, in the light of healing.

Socks

Weathered pegs attach to
winter's close line.
Socks, grey with red stripes
and red toes,
frozen in time.

Snow fills their opening, and nestles
in their stiff bent ankles; a
statement in this austere cold,
laughing, smiling; the beauty of
such a vignette, enriching a frigid morn.

Soon To Ash

Woodstove flames

stretch and reach,

catch and devour;

soon to ash.

How quickly our past,

can disappear, as if

it never happened.

Spirit Soars

Gracious and warm,
the send off,
the wake.

In time,
you are ash,
folded into earth.

Scars and all
complete a journey, while
spirit, soars forever.

Storm Rages

Night can be a lonely compartment, when
human connection sleeps, and
music, sleeps too.

Thoughts, louder than normal,
breath, closer to the surface, as
wind amplifies the silence within.

Candle's light dodge and dance on walls.
Shadows lick my heels, as
I walk the stairs , to stoke the fire.

House shudders, gusts pry at windows,
while trees moan and creak,
and the storm rages.

Sustenance

Above country road,
on wires strung taut,
from pole to pole,
Red Tailed hawk balances.

She bows, shoulders hunched,
primed for flight, to swoop
with talons splayed, catching
sustenance, under light of moon.

Tapestry

Is the bottom of grief abundance
or an acute sense of loss?
Reveal a deep pool of love, which

present and future will sustain.
Harrowing hurt that injures a soul, or
an ache that will not dissipate,

become stitches upon a tapestry,
worn and frayed, weaving the
language of journey.

Wear this mantle, this cloak.
Few will be able to read its testament;
treasure those who can.

Hold close the hearts
who know your gift,
rest in this knowledge of support.

Time will find and nurture. Breathe in
your angst, and breathe out,
the strength of your grace.

Tenderness of Dance

I wear your passion,

sense your closeness,

drink in your yearning.

Tenderness of dance,

dissolves in embrace,

lips in desire, touch . . .

The Dark Side of Light

The Alcoholic

I carry a heavy burden, a
burden of loss, that weighs my
heart into a rhythm of beating sorrow.

I mourn the loss of you; to yourself,
your talent, your creativity, and me.
But I am only peripheral damage.

How deep runs the river of this blight,
smashing against the rocks of resistance,
stones hurled, to snuff your candle, that

ebbs so low, I watch your light extinguish.
My anguish burns hot,
my breath sears open a scar that

bleeds into a pool of brackish dark,
a swirling vortex that has taken your soul;
that once took mine.

I witness your dance,
a dance all too familiar;
the dark side of light.

Discard the inertia which binds your spirit.
Fly with raven, run with brook.
Rise up with Phoenix, who will heal your soul.

The Door

I know not,
what lies within, or
why the urgency to discover.

I sense a chapter
unknown, and I
am beckoned to enter.

Padlock released, but
latch sticks with
hasp upon its hook.

Hinges squeak.
Barrel against flange
resists movement, while

door of oak, heavily
opposes entrance;
exit too perhaps?

Tentatively, I proceed.
The light is bright, and
I must stop, to breathe . . .

The Holidays

Within a slump, that
lifts and falls, in the
pit of thoughts,

never understood,
aggravated expectation resides in this
season, fraught with greed and want.

I speak gently to myself.
A void, a sorrow
consumes my core.

I have lost center.
I have lost balance.
I have lost my four legged companion.

The Journey

Autumn air,

sifts through

window sash,

gracing all the senses.

Soul transports,

deep within, a

place of peace and solitude.

Too infrequently, travels the mind

to such refuge.

Too often, we forget,

to welcome the journey.

The Shape of Water

In sand like ripples, of
varied spacing,
water freezes.

Cracking, crazing, with
cold's insistence,
translucent shifts to opaque,

with artistic order, and
considered detail.
Beneath this frozen surface,

giant amoeba play.
Air pockets, undulate and
pulse with brook's breath.

Brittle puddles,
fractured ponds,
endless artistry;

the shape of water.

Trio

In sunlit patches, lying,

on crisp Autumn morn,

Percheron three, curl and

nestle together.

Heavy vapour exits nostrils.

Gleaming velvet bodies,

black as ink, exude steam,

backlit by sun's warming rays.

Eyes, in gentle repose, close

against morning's light,

as day prepares

to sleep in unison, with

trio, black and radiant.

Utterances of Night

Listen,
to sounds of music, carried
upon the air of quiet night,
transported to place, an
entity of peace, of
introspection, of memory.

Breath slows, and life's blood,
beats notes of pathos and
empathy. Harmonic
minor, presents an
expression of emotion,
that will no longer fit,

between ribs of protection, where
chest walls swell with thought and gesture.
Breathe into this opportunity of knowing,
absorb the limitless boundary of self, the
power of strength and resilience, all carried,
upon the utterances of night.

Visitor of the Night

Fluttering in vane,
juvenile bird, struggles
at my window pane.

Effort endures, on narrow sill,
breath laboured, 'till
scuffle relents to exhaust will.

Motionless is my guest,
lost and missing from her brood,
anxious little one left to rest.

Suddenly, at first light,
departs wee bird from ledge so steep,
my tired visitor of the night.

Witness

Water pools and eddies
around beach rock, as
tide recedes,

pulling with it, the
sands of time,
leaving declivities,

in front of stones,
in front of gulls,
in front of me.

Tiny mollusk shells
dot this canvas with
dime sized jelly dollops; scattered

upon this wide expanse, which
speaks of rhythm, calm and order.
Witness, the gifts of the sea.

9 789363 543720